ADVENTURES
in Songwriting

A Guide For Kids
—And Anyone Who Wants
To Write Songs

By Gina Boe & Sue C. Smith

Illustrated by Sue C. Smith

To all the budding songwriters out there
who are eager to learn.
And to my own kids, Hunter, Hannah, Harrison, and Houston;
I pray you each write the unique and beautiful song
in your own heart.
—Gina Boe

To Lauren and Mark, Alex and Garrett,
and Jacob, Houston,
Hudson, and Violet.
You are my favorite kids on the planet.
I pray you'll always let God write your life song.
—Sue C. Smith

Adventures In Songwriting
A Guide For Kids—And Anyone
Who Wants To Write Songs

Copyright © 2017 Gina Boe & Sue C. Smith

ISBN-10: 0-9991802-0-7
ISBN: 978-0-9991802-0-4

Because of the dynamic nature of the Internet, any web addresses or links contained in this book may have changed since publication and may no longer be valid. The views expressed in this work are solely those of the authors.

Middle C Books
an imprint of
One Accord Gospel Productions, Inc.
PO Box 1364
St. Charles, MO 63302

TABLE OF CONTENTS

INTRODUCTION

YOU CAN WRITE A SONG

Get Ready For The Life-long Adventure Of Songwriting

Welcome to the wonderful world of songwriting!

If you are reading this book, chances are you have already written a
song, or you think it would be fun
to try. Either way, you have
embarked on an amazing
journey!

Songs are all around us almost
all the time. It's hard to go
through an entire day without
hearing at least one song,
whether you're in your house, at
school, or in your car. Chances
are you can think of a song that
has stuck with you for a long
time. It may be something your
mom or dad sang to you when
you were very little. It may be a
song you learned in church. Or it
may be something you heard on
the radio. Songs are everywhere
and they stick in our brains like
nothing else can!

Songs are simply a creative way to communicate a message, story, emotion, or opinion. You've probably heard thousands of songs in your lifetime, but have you thought much about the people who wrote those songs? Songwriters are basically artists who have the unique ability to create little pieces of artwork that have the power to do amazing things. Songs can inspire us, give us new information, help us express emotion, and move us to action. It's a pretty cool thing to be a songwriter.

So exactly who can write a song? Well, anyone! If you've got something to say, then a song might be the perfect way to say it.

You don't have to be a certain age. You don't even need to be able to play an instrument. However, there are some basic principles to songwriting, and like any other skill, learning how to write songs and do it well does take some time and effort.

We hope this book will teach you some basics about songwriting, give you some tools and exercises to improve your writing, and also help you to develop good songwriting habits and a songwriting support system. So, if you're ready to dive into this songwriting adventure, let's get started!

Gina & Sue

CHAPTER 1

COOKING UP A SONG

Discovering the Ingredients For A Great Song

Have you seen that TV show where chefs are given a basket of four ingredients and they have to make a dish using them? Sometimes the basket has items in it you've never even heard of, and you sure wouldn't know what to do with them to make something that tasted good. But the chefs on the show always seem to have an idea of how to take those four items and add other ingredients to them to create something creative and delicious. They're chefs and they know how to cook.

Just like a chef needs to know about ingredients, how they taste, what the texture is like, and how they'll work with other ingredients, songwriters work with basic "ingredients" to cook up a song. When you're just starting to write, some of the ingredients to a song may be a little unfamiliar to you, but as you keep practicing, you'll learn how to work with all of them.

Here are the basics about the basics:

IDEAS

Songs almost always start with an idea. What do you want to write about? What do you want to say? What do people want to hear or need to hear? What's stirring in your heart and mind? We'll say

more about ideas in another chapter, but just know that it's almost impossible to have a great song without a great idea.

GENRE

This may be a strange word to you but you already know what it means. Take a look at the iTunes store and you'll see a whole list of categories, from pop to rock to country to hip hop and more. Those are all musical genres. Think about the cereal aisle at the grocery store. There are cereals for every taste, age, and nutritional need. Genres are like that. You'll probably start out writing songs that fit the genre you listen to most. But there's no reason you can't try other genres. What kinds of songs do you want to write?

If you know someone named Tanya, the word "genre" rhymes with that. Start it with the sound you would make if you combined a "j" with an "sh." A good way to think about a song's "genre" is the label you might use to describe its category.

STRUCTURE

There's a lot to say about structure and we'll take another chapter
to do it. Just remember that structure isn't just a list of rules about

what you should or shouldn't do in a song. Good structure helps
the audience know what's happening in a song. It makes a song
stronger because it's put together in a way that makes sense.

LYRIC

The lyric is the words of the song. Words are powerful. They make
you think and feel. There are words to songs rattling around in
your brain right now. You might have learned them when you were
very small, but they're still there. Chances are you can find them
and bring them right back to the front. There are other words that
you've just heard, but because they made you feel something,
your mind is already storing them away for the future.

MELODY

The melody is the way the notes go up and down in pitch and the tempo and rhythm they use to do it. Just like the words make you feel a certain way, the melody of a song makes you feel too. If it's a happy song, the melody will make you have that sunny feeling in your heart. If a song is meant to be sad or lonely or tragic or mysterious, the melody says that to you just as clearly as the words do. It's why we use songs to cheer us up or help us cry. We listen to them when we're missing someone and when we want to get a crowd excited. Melodies are powerful tools to make us feel what the writer wants us to feel.

These are the basic ingredients of a song. The more you know about these basics and how to make them work together, the better your songs are going to be.

Helpful Tip

Even though songwriting is an actual job for some people, they would be the first to tell you that it's supposed to be fun! So, no stressing allowed about songwriting. Have fun. Try stuff you've never done. Nobody's judging.

TRY IT OUT

1. To understand more about how song ingredients work, write down the titles to five of your favorite songs and then write the big idea of each song. Try to write the idea in a complete sentence. For example, the big idea of "God Bless America" might be "I love America and pray that God will bless it."

2. Look on iTunes at the link called "All Genres." List three genres that are your favorites. Look at the Top Songs in each one. How many of the Top Songs do you know?

3. List three genres that you don't listen to but might want to try. Look at the Top Songs in each one and write down some titles that seem interesting. Now listen to a clip of each of the songs and react. What did you think about these songs? Does the lyric appeal to you? Are you interested in the melody?

Chapter 2

Construction Zone

Why Good Structure Is a Great Way To Begin

Think of this: There are about 80 LEGO pieces for every human being on our planet! Kids all over the world spend 5 billion hours each year playing with LEGO bricks. It's the most popular toy in the world. Maybe that's because people, and kids especially, love creating and building.

Creating and building are what songwriting is all about. It's taking the elements that we talked about in Chapter 1 and making something exciting and beautiful with them.

Even though it is a very creative thing to do, songs usually are better if the writers follow some guidelines for putting them together. It's what's called "structure." It's fun to make a LEGO building that's all crazy and off balance. But those don't usually stand up very well. If you want to build something that will last, good structure is the way to make sure that happens.

If you're building a house—and would you believe that someone actually did build a real house out of LEGO—, you start with a foundation.

You may have learned a song when you were small that said, "The wise man built his house upon the rock." Well, building on a firm foundation makes sense, whether you're building a house or a song.

Once you've got that foundation, you probably want walls. You want a roof and doors and windows. Getting the walls straight and connected in a way that makes sense and putting the roof on so it doesn't cave in are all important in the building process.

Let's take a look at what good structure looks like in a song. Let's say the foundation is the great idea you start with. Once you've got the idea, then you make more choices about what your song is going to be like.

THE VERSES AND THE CHORUS

These days, most songs you hear on the radio start with something called the verse. After the verse, most songs have what's called a chorus. Then you can kind of expect to hear another verse. The melody for the second verse is almost always the same as the first verse. It sounds just the same, but the words are different.

After the second verse, you hear the chorus again, and it has the same melody it did the first time and almost always the same words too.

This kind of structure looks like this in a songwriter's brain:

VERSE
CHORUS
VERSE
CHORUS

A good example of this kind of song is "The Battle Hymn Of The Republic," lyric by Julia Ward Howe. When you listen, you'll hear three different verses, but after each verse you will hear the chorus ("Glory, glory hallelujah..."). Not many current songs are verse-chorus-verse-chorus, but you may still sing some hymns at church that have this structure.

That's just one kind of song structure.

BUILD A BRIDGE

Maybe you've listened to songs that get to the end of the second chorus, and then they start a new melody that hasn't been part of the song before. Then the next thing you know, you're hearing that chorus again. Songwriters call that new part the bridge. It is a very familiar song structure to songwriters that looks like this:

VERSE
CHORUS
VERSE
CHORUS
BRIDGE
CHORUS

A good example of this kind of song is "You Can't Take That," written by Gina Boe and Sue C. Smith. You can listen to it and see the lyric at adventuresinsongwriting.org.

SONGS WITH A PRE-CHORUS

Some songs add in a little extra section that comes between the verse and the chorus, and it goes by more than one name. Most of the time, it's called the pre-chorus. In other words, it sort of introduces the chorus. Usually the pre-chorus is just a line or two. It's shorter than the verse and the chorus. You could almost think of it as a little "hallway" in the song "house" you are constructing that connects the bedrooms with the great room. The structure would look like this:

VERSE
PRE-CHORUS
CHORUS
VERSE
PRE-CHORUS
CHORUS
BRIDGE
CHORUS

A good example of this kind of song is "Give A Little Love Away," by Gina Boe and Sue C. Smith. You can listen to it and see the lyric at adventurersinsongwriting.org.

LEAVING OUT THE CHORUS

There's a third kind of structure that you'll hear occasionally. It looks like this:

VERSE
VERSE
BRIDGE
VERSE

One good example of this kind of song is "Listen My Children," by Gina Boe and Sue C. Smith. Listen to it and see the lyric at adventuresinsongwriting.org.

There's not even a chorus in this kind of song. For that reason, you won't usually hear a song like this on pop radio these days. Radio listeners seem to really love a big chorus that they can learn quickly and sing at the top of their lungs.

This kind of song is different. In this kind of song structure, the last line of each verse is usually the same words and melody, and it usually is the title or what we call the "hook" of the song.

The "hook" is a memorable phrase that gets repeated in a song, usually in the chorus. Often the hook is also the title, and sometimes it also makes the main idea clear. After all, what better way for the writer to help you remember it than to repeat it!

WHEN THE VERSE IS EVERYTHING

There's still another kind of song structure that looks like this:

VERSE
VERSE
VERSE
VERSE

A good example of this kind of song is "Silent Night," melody by Franz Gruber, lyric by Joseph Mohr.

In this structure, there's no chorus. And no bridge. There are just verses, and often the verses are 4 lines. If you've spent much time singing in church, you'll recognize this kind of structure as what is used in many classic hymns. But don't make the mistake of thinking this structure is only for hymns. It has been used in other kinds of songs too, like old folk songs and ballads that told stories of historic events.

Keep your eyes and ears open for all these song structures. Remember, every song you listen to is a chance to learn.

Once you've started recognizing song structures, you'll want to learn some very basic rules that songwriters often follow:

1. The big idea (the hook) of the song is almost always in the chorus. Sometimes it's at the beginning and at the end of the chorus. Sometimes it's just at the end. But most of the time, that's where you can expect to find it.

2. Verse one gets the listener ready to hear the big idea in the chorus.

3. Verse two gets the listener ready to hear the chorus again, but in a different way with a different approach or different ideas than verse one did.

4. Verse one and verse two use the same music, but even though the words are different, they "sing" the same.

That's all pretty simple, right? Those are the basics of structure. Now, we're ready to build!

Helpful Tip

You can learn what makes a song successful by paying attention to what is going in songs you love. Write down the lyric and listen as you watch the words to see if you can recognize the different parts of the structure —the verse, the chorus, the pre-chorus (if there is one), the bridge (if there is one).

TRY IT OUT

1. Start listening to songs and making a collection of the different song structures you hear. If you have some CD's, you might even look at the lyric in the tray card, if it's included. Looking at the lyric as you listen is a good way to start to recognize song structures.

2. Write down the lyric to your favorite song and then identify the parts of the song: verse 1, the chorus, verse 2, the bridge (if there is one). Now listen to the song and write down how the parts seem different to you.

3. Listen to the 3 songs written for this book at adventuresinsongwriting.org. Without looking at the lyric, see if you can identify the structure of each song. Now look at the lyric to see if you were right.

CHAPTER 3

DAREDEVILS WANTED

Where Song Ideas Hide and How To Find Them

In the classic book, *The Hobbit*, by J.R.R. Tolkien, Bilbo Baggins is offered the chance to leave his home in the shire and join Gandalf the Wizard and a group of dwarves as they set out on a journey to reclaim the dwarves' kingdom. At first, Bilbo refuses the offer. A short while later, he has a change of heart and decides to join the group, not having a clue what awaits him.

In a favorite scene from the movie version of The Hobbit, Bilbo is shown running from his home to catch up with the group. As he is running, he hollers out with excitement to his neighbor, "I'm going on an adventure!" In many ways, songwriting should feel like that.

Songwriting requires work. Great songs don't just drop down from the sky into our brains while we sit around watching TV and eating junk food. It takes discipline and effort to discover new things to write about. But if you approach this process with a sense of adventure, songwriting will be a whole lot more fun.

Sometimes we need to be reminded of all the places new ideas are just waiting to be discovered. Here are a few suggestions of where you can look.

YOUR DIARY OR JOURNAL

Keeping a record of what you do on a regular basis is a great way to stash away thoughts to come back to at another time. While they may not seem too exciting as you're writing them down, re-reading through them later might trigger an idea for a new song. You may begin to see patterns or repeated themes. These make good song ideas. You can also try writing out what is bothering you, what you are worrying about, or what you are praying for. Journaling can be a great resource for song ideas.

PEOPLE

One of the best resources for song ideas is found in all the people around us. There are ideas in the things they say, the things they do, and the stories they live and tell. You can write about how you feel about someone special in your life. Maybe someone you know has had an amazing or rewarding experience of some kind and you could tell about it in a song.

Sometimes, the people we love go through hard things, and a song is a perfect way to encourage them. By paying close attention to the conversations we have with family and friends, we can find subjects to write about or even little phrases to incorporate into our songs.

HOBBIES

What do you like to do in your spare time? Do you play sports, watch movies, or work on cars? Whatever it is, you can certainly write a song about it. No matter the activity, if it's something you enjoy and maybe are good at, you're already the perfect person to write about it.

THE NEWS AND SOCIAL MEDIA

There are true stories around us every day, and they can inspire a song. Watch for unusual and interesting stories in the news and imagine what the people in them are thinking and feeling. Pay attention to letters to advice columnists and letters to the editor. Even cartoons and comics may have a nugget of an idea.

Social media is a great place to look for ideas. What people post on Facebook, Twitter, or Instagram may be phrased in a way that is song idea. Learn to "read like a writer," as if everything has the potential to be the source of your next song.

BOOKS, MOVIES, MUSIC, AND ART

Sometimes we need to spend time enjoying someone else's creativity to be inspired to do our own creative work. By reading books, watching movies, listening to music, or enjoying different kinds of art, we can find endless ideas of what to write about. Capture ideas that spark your interest as you read, listen, or watch, by writing them down. Don't let them disappear.

TRY IT OUT

1. Choose a new kind of creative work to enjoy. Go to a ballet, watch a documentary, or read a book you wouldn't normally pick up. Choose something you haven't done before. When you're done, see if you can write down some things you might want to write a song about.

2. To start stockpiling ideas to write, make a list that includes: A person or persons you could write a song about. It could be someone living or dead, someone you know or someone who just interests you. List a place that is important to you, a place you've never been that interests you, and a place you'd never want to visit. List an invention that has changed your life, something you own that is a "treasure," and something you really need to throw away— but you don't. List an event in your life that you'll never forget, a memory that makes you smile, and a memory that is painful. Write down something people do that drives you crazy, a goal you'd like to achieve before your next birthday, a dream for the future, and a secret wish you've never told anyone else. Finally, list your favorite part of your day, and then your least favorite part. Now just look at all the ideas that could become your next song!

CHAPTER 4

HARNESSING THE HURRICANE

Writing The Words To Your Song

You came into the world as a tiny baby, not knowing a single word. But before you ever went to school, you had mastered getting what you wanted with words you had learned just by listening and experimenting. Your first words may be on video somewhere because they were so thrilling to your parents. Then you learned to say "No!" and "Why?" and all kinds of other words. By the time you were 8 years old, you knew at least 10,000 words!

While it's true that some songs are just melody, when you add words to a song, it's like you multiply its power to move the listener's emotions. The melody and the lyric work as a team to make the listener feel what you want them to feel.

The average song has somewhere between 100-300 words. So even if you only have the vocabulary of an 8-year-old, you've still got some big choices to make: Which words are the right ones to use?

In the chapter where we talked about structure, we said that usually the big idea of the song is in the chorus. This is a good time to begin working on how you will say your idea in the chorus in words that have a big impact.

Sometimes the idea itself will be said in very simple words like "Life is beautiful." But the words that lead up to saying that hook

Helpful Tip

Spend all the time you need to working on your hook. The reason it's called a hook is because you're going to "hang" the rest of your song on it!

get the listener ready to hear it. Sometimes the hook is a group of words that just make you remember them.

Okay. You've got your idea, You've got your hook. You've got a bunch of things you want to say. Now, how do you choose the right words to say them?

Here is where songwriting becomes a little like working a big puzzle. Let's say you've decided on this structure:

VERSE
CHORUS
VERSE
CHORUS

Maybe now is a good time to figure out where you're going to use the hook. Will you start and end the chorus with it? Will you start

Helpful Tip

Once again, all the songs you love are good teachers. Where do you see the hook used in them?

the chorus with it and then use it again halfway through? Will the hook only be heard at the end of the chorus?

BALANCE AND CONTRAST

If you know how to ride a bike, you know that balance is important. Balance in your song can mean balance between the verses and the chorus. It could mean balance between simple and complex. It could mean balance between lots of words and few words. If there's too much interest and "weight" in one part of the song and not enough in another, the song may seem unbalanced.

Just like being too "matchy" is not the greatest in fashion, you don't want to be so "matchy" in your song that it's boring. That means that in addition to balance, you'll want contrast in your song. If your verses are long and wordy, your chorus may be short and simple. If your verse makes the listener think hard, maybe the chorus will give them a chance to just rest on one repeated phrase. This is how songwriters use contrast in the songs they write. It's something that will be different in every song and something you will get a feeling for as you write.

RHYME

You learned to rhyme in pre-school, and so this part of songwriting should be fun and easy. But there may be more to rhyming than you might have imagined.

Once you've come up with a pattern of rhymes for your song, stick with it. For example, if your first verse has rhymes on the first and second lines and then on the third and fourth lines, you should use that pattern in other verses. Songwriters would call that an A-A-B-B rhyme. Just follow the pattern you have set up in each verse you write. The chorus is different, and it can have its own rhyme pattern.

There are perfect rhymes, like might, right, tight, fight. And then there are imperfect rhymes. Sometimes they're called near rhymes. Some examples would be might, like, life, and wide. Those words don't rhyme exactly, but when they are sung, they are close enough to sound like rhymes to a listener.

Why use imperfect or close rhymes? Because using close rhymes gives you many more words to choose from. As you begin writing more songs, you will probably start noticing interesting rhymes more than ever. It might be fun to keep a file of them, because saving them will help you think of fresh creative rhymes too.

COUNTING SYLLABLES

Here's another guideline for writing lyrics: It's often a good idea to make your verses match. You're already learning it's a good idea to use the same rhyme pattern. It's also helpful to make your verses match when it comes to the number of lines, and even the

number of syllables in the lines. If line one of verse one has 7 syllables, it's usually a good idea to have 7 syllables in line one of verse two. If line two of verse one has 6 syllables, line two of verse two should match. And so on.

DOING ACCENTS RIGHT

Finding where words are accented is just taking your syllable matching one more step. Often songwriters try to match the rhythm of accented and unaccented syllables in corresponding lines. Always try to write so that the words "sing" with the same accented syllables you use to "say" those words.

For example: Think of how you say these words: because, funny, anything, creation.

Do you hear the natural rhythm of the words? It would sound odd to say "because" with the accent on the "be-" part of the word, wouldn't it? But it would sound just as strange to accent the "-ny" in the word "funny." Pay attention to which syllables are accented and make them "sing" that way.

"Syntax" (pronounced "sin-tax") means arranging your words to make your message clear. In songwriting, it's usually good to put your words in the same order you would if you just said the idea to someone.

SYNTAX

Sometimes beginning songwriters turn the phrasing of a sentence around because they are trying to rhyme two lines and that's the only way they know how to do it. If you know the character of Yoda in the Star Wars movies, that's the way he speaks.

Conversational word order: I feel like I could fly.

Yoda-speak: Fly I could I feel.

Conversational word order: I really want to be your friend.

Yoda-speak: To be your friend I really want.

People who make their living writing songs avoid Yoda-speak like crazy. They make the word order sound the way people really talk.

Writing the words to a song can be basic and simple. On the other hand, some people spend their whole writing career learning how to write the lyric better and better.

Helpful Tip

"Practice makes perfect" is absolutely true when it comes to songwriting. The more you do it, the better you will get!

TRY IT OUT

1. Find a simple song you like that has verses that are just 4-lines. Write a new verse to the song. Try to use perfect rhymes, match the syllables, get the accents right, and avoid Yoda-speak! (Remember this is just for practice. It is against the law to change the words of another writer's song and make it public without permission!)

2. Listen to "Give A Little Love Away" at adventuresinsongwriting.org and study the lyric. List all the examples of perfect rhymes you can find. Now find examples of imperfect rhymes.

3. Look at the 4 verses to "Children Listen" at adventuresinsongwriting.org. Count the syllables in each line of verse 1 and write them down. Now count the syllables in each line of the other 3 verses. Do the syllables in each first line of the other verses match the first line of verse 1? Do the syllables in each of the lines of the other verses match the corresponding line in verse 1?

CHAPTER 5

PLAYING WITH WORDS

Getting Creative With Your Lyric

A student from another country who didn't speak English very well was talking with an American student. At one point in the conversation, the American student joked, "Oh you're just pulling my leg."

Now, all of us would understand that he was saying, "You're trying to fool me" or maybe "You're joking."

The other student got very upset and said, "Oh no. I was not touching you. I am so sorry!"

Sometimes the expressions we use in English just don't make sense if you haven't heard them before. There are probably expressions like this in other languages that would be just as confusing to us.

That's the way language works. We have all kinds of ways of using our words to make someone see or hear or feel what we mean.

The ways we play with words are called "literary expressions." There are all kinds of these, and we could spend a lot of time giving you a definition of each one and telling you examples. You'll probably learn many of them as you go through school. The important thing is for you to notice the way they work and to learn how to use them to bring life to your songs.

Which is more interesting: I was really really really angry!

Or: My anger burned like a volcano that felt like it could explode through the top of my head.

Is it more vivid to say: *The night sky was black and it was filled with stars.*

Or: *A million bright stars sparkled like diamonds on the black velvet sky.*

See the difference?

There are dozens of kinds of literary expressions, but if you will just think about some general categories, it will help you use them.

"Literary devices." These are techniques writers use to make their work more interesting and vivid. There are many devices like this. We've included some broad categories in this book.

COMPARISONS

We use comparisons all the time to express ourselves. Maybe you have said "I am as hungry as a horse." Or "My hair looks like a bird's nest."

Those are a kind of comparison we all use so much that we don't even think about it.

You already use comparisons without really thinking about it. Now is the time to start collecting the interesting, fun, and powerful comparisons you hear and to start creating some of your own.

What does joy look like to you?

What color is joy?

What does joy sound like?

What place says sadness to you?

What does sadness sound like?

EXAGGERATIONS

Another way we play with language is by using exaggerations to make our point. We say we're so tired we could fall asleep standing up. We say the roof is caving in when things are going wrong. We say that someone is as old as the hills or that we have a ton of homework.

Exaggerations can work in songs too if you use them right. Here are some in recent pop songs:

Cry me a river.

I would fly to the moon and back.

It's raining men.

I jumped so high I touched the clouds.

See how exaggerated these statements are? We don't really expect a river to gush from someone's eyes. And if it started raining people, well, that would be a huge news story! But the exaggeration helps us get the point, doesn't it?

WORD SOUNDS

We all understand rhymes.

We've already mentioned that some rhymes are perfect, like "night, bright, light, fright." Some rhymes are close rhymes, like "love, was, tough, but."

There are only a few perfect rhymes for "God," like "sod, clod, nod, rod." But if you use close rhymes, you might choose a word

Rhyme

bat	sing	*would*
hat	thing	*could*
cat	ring	*should*
rat	wing	*good*

like "thought" or "job," or even "loss" and "cross." It's fun to make your rhyme bank bigger just by learning to use close rhymes.

There's another way of using word sounds. Listen to words like "buzz," "clink," "ring," and "giggle." When you hear those words, they sound like what they mean.

Try thinking of the sounds of words as you write and try to match their sounds to what you are writing about.

DESCRIPTIONS

As songwriters, we need to learn how to describe people, places, situations, and especially feelings. A big part of that is simply noticing the world around you. Notice the colors, lights, sights, sounds, feelings, changes in the weather, and changes in your feelings. Notice the way great writers describe these things, and then start trying out your own descriptions. You don't need fancy words. You just want to choose the right words.

Your goal in playing with words is to make the person listening to your song feel what you want them to feel. That means that you have to decide what you want them to feel.

You don't make people feel an emotion by telling them to feel it. If I say to you "laugh," you might try a sort of laugh, but you won't feel what people feel when they really laugh. The way to do that is to tell you a funny joke or show you a funny video.

Helpful Tip

As you are writing, "show, don't tell." Paint a picture with your words that will cause someone to feel happy, sad, excited, peaceful—whatever you want them to feel.

TRY IT OUT

1. Do a brain dump on one of the ideas you plan to write. List at least 50 words. See if any of them are close rhymes or near rhymes. Take 10 of the words and see how many rhyming words you can write down. Be as playful with your list as you want. Even if a word doesn't seem like it would be at home in a song, you just never know.

2. Look at the lyric for "You Can't Take That" at adventuresinsongwriting.org. Find examples of slang phrases or catch-phrases. Clue: One is "sticks and stones" in the bridge. You might be able to find 8 more.

CHAPTER 6

MAKING IT SING

Coming Up With A Memorable Melody

Now that you've learned more about working with words, it's time to talk about the other half of what makes a song. A song isn't really a song if it only has a lyric. The words by themselves are sort of like a poem. But, when you put those words to a sequence of musical notes, Then you've got a song. That sequence of musical notes is called the melody, and connecting the words to the perfect melody is very important in your quest to write something great.

BE MEMORABLE

You've probably found yourself humming a tune without even really thinking about it. Soon, you realize you're humming the melody to a song that you've recently heard and now it's stuck in your head. A great melody does that. It sticks with you.

So what is it about certain melodies that we can't seem to get out of our head? There are a few things that make a melody memorable, and it is helpful for songwriters to remember these things as we try to write songs people will want to hear.

BE HOOKY

There should be a melodic hook, something repetitive or catchy that the listener just can't help but sing along to. The melodic hook can be something musical, as in a certain succession of notes, or, something rhythmic, like a pattern that repeats. Whatever kind of hook it is, it usually appears several times in the song. Think of the songs "Mary Had A Little Lamb" and "Twinkle, Twinkle Little Star." Sing them a few times and listen for how many little phrases repeat, both the notes and the rhythmic pattern. There is a lot of repetition. That's one of the reasons those songs are so recognizable.

BE SINGABLE

The melody should be fun or easy to sing. People love to sing along with their favorite songs. Not everyone has the perfect voice to sing along with every song they like, but the more the melody stays within a certain range of notes, the more it helps someone who is not a professional singer. Try to keep the melody of a song within an octave to one and a half octaves of a musical scale. Then the range of the song won't go too high or too low for the average person to sing along.

Another thing to consider when writing melody is the rise and fall of the song. Usually, the melody in the verses of the song is a little lower in the range. As the song goes along, the melody might go up. When you get to the chorus, the notes are a little higher in the range. If there's a bridge, the melody might even go higher. All of those moments when the melody rises and falls help create some kind of emotional response when the listener hears them. The melody can build excitement, give an emotional payoff to a lyric, or resolve the tension created in another part of the song.

USE PATTERNS

If you pay attention to melodies, you will find that they are full of

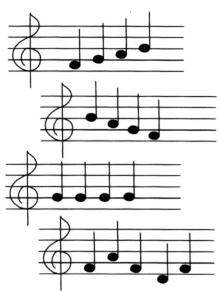

patterns. Sometimes the melody will go up in a series of steps. Sometimes it will go down in steps. That's a pattern. Sometimes the same note will repeat several times. That's a pattern called repetition. Other times the melody will take leaps over notes. When you hear that happen in the same way more than once, you've found another pattern. Paying attention to patterns will help you see how a great melody works.

These are a few of the guidelines you can pay attention to when writing your melodies. Remember that these are not unbreakable rules. The important thing is creating the right melody for the right lyric. When you find the perfect fit, then you've got a great song.

Once you've gained a better understanding about what makes a good melody, you can spend some time taking a closer look at how a melody fits into the big picture of a song, and lining it up with the chords used throughout the song. Try looking up a favorite song of yours online. Use Google to see if you can find what is called a "lead sheet" for it. The lead sheet will show you the notes that make up the melody, as well as the chords used throughout the song.

It's like a puzzle you can study to see how it all fits together.

Helpful Tip

If you learn to play the songs you like, it will help you understand more clearly how great melodies work. You don't have to be a great musician to just find the notes of a melody on a keyboard.

TRY IT OUT

1. Melody Mapping – Get a piece of paper and a pencil. Listen to three different songs. As you listen, draw a line across the paper from left to right. As the melody goes up and down, make your line go up and down across the page. Notice where the high and low points are in the songs. You can even write on the song map where the verses and choruses are. It's fun to see what happens to the melody in the different sections of the songs!

2. Listen to two of the songs written for this book. You will find them at adventuresinsongwriting.org. Identify any patterns you hear: ascending (going up) phrases, descending (going down) phrases, repetition of one note, or something else. Where is the melodic hook? How does the title or topic of the song prepare you for the melody you are going to hear?

CHAPTER 7

IT'S BETTER WITH FRIENDS

How To Be A Great Co-writer

You could write a song by yourself. You totally could.

But guess what? There's something really cool about writing with other people.

Here's why we think co-writing is a great idea:

1. When 2 or 3 people work on a song together, they combine the things they are good at. They also make up for each other's weaknesses.

2. When you have decided on a time to co-write with someone, you don't put it off like you do sometimes when you have to sit down all by yourself and write. You show up.

3. When you co-write, you get to hear what other people think about important things in life, and you have someone to listen to what you think. You learn to express yourself, your beliefs, and the things that matter most to you.

4. Co-writing is just fun!

So how does a typical co-write work?

In a professional co-write, the writers often make an appointment to get together. They might meet at the company one of them writes for or at somebody's home or even at a coffee shop. They'll sit down in a little room. Maybe they'll have a cup of coffee or a snack. They'll chat about what's going on in their lives for a little while. If they haven't written together before, they might spend a little time getting to know each other. But after a while, one of them will ask, "Well, what do you want to write about today?"

That question will start the writers tossing out their ideas. They'll listen closely to each other. They'll discuss each idea. They'll talk about what it means to them, and how it makes them feel. Sooner or later, they'll decide on one idea.

After that, a co-write can go many directions. The writers may spend time deciding on the "hook" of the song. They might "map" the song out by deciding things the chorus could say and how the verses will get the listeners ready to hear the chorus. Sometimes they'll start with the melody. They'll play with different melodies and try to get a feel for what would sound good.

A "professional songwriter" is anyone who makes all or part of his or her income from writing songs. There's more information about how this happens in Chapter 9 of this book.

Sometimes one writer will work just on the lyric, and the other writer or writers will write the melody. But more often, the writers will work together.

The important thing to know is there's no one right way or wrong way. Every co-write can look different.

It's also important to be a good co-writer. Here are some co-writing rules we think are important:

1. Respect
2. Honesty
3. Kindness
4. Listening
5. Courage
6. Caring

DO BE RESPECTFUL. Respect other people's time. If you say you're going to write at a certain time, be there. Respect ideas. When someone shares an idea, remember how scary it can be when it's your turn. React the way you'd like others to react to you. Respect what happens in the writing room. Don't leave and talk bad about your co- writers. Don't make fun of something silly they said. Don't share personal stories they've told you.

DO BE HONEST. If you're going to write, the truth is that sometimes—

well, lots of times—you're not going to get your way. As a writer, you're going to hear the word "no" more often than you hear "yes." But in the co-writing room, you have to be honest. If something isn't as good as it might be, have the courage to talk about it.

DO BE KIND. This is so important. If you are unkind, it makes for a terrible co-write. People quit sharing. They quit trying. They just want to get out of there. This is where the Golden Rule is so important. Even when you have to be honest and disagree on something, do it in a way that is kind. A good way to do this is to make it like a little "sandwich." Start with something good: "I really like the way your idea is truthful and just what people say." Then go to the thing that might be harder to hear: "But I think there are other songs that have said this exact thing. I wonder if we could find another way to say this." And finally end with something positive: "This idea is so good that I'm excited to see what we can come up with if we keep working."

DO LISTEN. Listening may be one of the most important things you do as a co-writer. Really listen to what your co-writers are saying. In discussing the idea, they might say something great and they don't even realize they've said it. But if you're really listening, you might hear the perfect thing the song needs to say.

SPEAK YOUR MIND. The easiest thing is to let

everybody else take the risk of offering their thoughts and ideas. It's scary to share what you think. But if everyone in the co-write cares about others and cares about the song, you will have the right approach.

CARE ABOUT PEOPLE more than the song. Songs are important and it is great to start a song, or finish a song, or hear your song sung by someone. But nothing is more important than the friendships you will make because of songwriting. People matter most of all.

When you follow these rules, you will find that people like getting together with you. They'll like writing with you. And you'll accomplish more than you ever dreamed you would!

Helpful Tip

Being a good co-writer is simply a lot like being a good friend. Be thoughtful, kind, and loyal inside the writing room and out of it.

TRY IT OUT

1. Make a list of possible co-writers and talk to one or two of them about the idea of writing together. Share what you are learning from this book or encourage them to get their own copy.

2. Make your first co-writing appointment and then, just do it! Bring several possible song ideas with you, talk through them, and try to get started on your first co-written song. At the end of your co-writing time, set up your next co-write.

CHAPTER 8

SECOND-CHANCE WRITING

When, Why, and How To Re-write Your Song

Have you ever been playing a game with friends when someone shouts out "do over!" That's when they get the chance to do whatever they've just done again. And hopefully, they do it better than they did the first time. We get to do that as songwriters too. Those "do-overs" are what the rewriting process is all about.

Someone very wise once said, "Writing is rewriting." If you really want to be a great songwriter, you must be willing to make changes to your songs when doing that could make them better.

REASONS TO REWRITE

If you are writing songs for other people to sing, chances are you'll have to play your song for a publisher first. A publisher might love your song, but there are more things to think about than just whether or not he or she likes listening to it. The publisher has to think about things like the length of the song, how the song might appeal to the radio audience, how much range the singer has, and where the song might fit on a particular album. In light of all those things, the publisher might ask you to make changes to the song to fit certain guidelines.

You might need to make the song shorter, which could mean rewriting the lyric and melody. You might need to make the range smaller so a certain singer can sing it. That would require a rewrite of the melody. Sometimes you'll take a song that you wrote with a slower tempo and change it up to be a faster song.

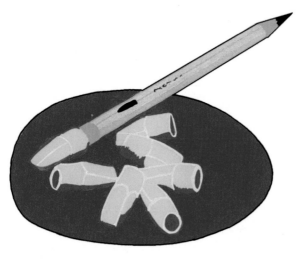

Occasionally you might have the opportunity to write for a particular artist. When an artist hears a song, they have to think about how it fits when they sing the song in their concerts. They also have to consider if it works well with the rest of the songs on their album. They might love the song, but some of the words you used in the lyric aren't the vocabulary or style of conversation they might use. They might ask for a rewrite for any of these reasons.

Sometimes you'll finish a song, set it aside for a while, then come back to it later and think, "Well, that doesn't sound right." It's a good idea to revisit your songs occasionally and see if something strikes you that might need to be changed. We all become a little wiser the more songs we write. Making another attempt at an older song can be fun.

HOW TO RE-WRITE

One reason we rewrite is because the message isn't clear. Try writing the main idea of the song at the top of your lyric page. Then you can go through the lyric line by line to make sure everything helps you say the main idea.

IDEA: YOUR LOVE CAN CHANGE THE WORLD
a little

Give Love Away — Hook

Vs1 How do you make a difference change the world?
When things seem hopeless it is what it is
Where do you start — make your
When the world is so big? mark
you're only one voice

Chorus Give yourself away love
a little LOVE

Take a little time to say and do
The things that you
Want somebody to do for you
One spark — can light a heart
Can set the world on fire — flame?
(50) Let's start. ablaze?
To give love away
(a little)

Often a first draft of a song is too long because you try to fit too much information in the song. Go through the song and take out any words or phrases that aren't necessary to communicate the main idea. If you narrow the focus of the message, you might find out you have enough information for two songs.

Rewriting can feel like doing a puzzle. You might have all the right pieces, but they just need to be moved around a little bit. If the lyric isn't clear, try moving some lines around or putting verses in a different order to see if that helps.

If the lyric isn't interesting or creative enough, try putting in more word pictures. For example, instead of saying "I went to the store," you might say "I wandered the cobblestone streets to the corner stop-n-shop." A thesaurus can also be helpful to find some different words to use.

Once you have a melody stuck in your head, it can be hard to write something different. Rewriting melodies often means a lot of trial and error. Try to be as brave and creative as you can when rewriting. Record yourself singing different melodies for a lyric and you just might stumble upon something amazing! To make the melody more interesting, try using some different chords underneath the same melody. This might mean becoming more familiar with music theory so you understand your options.

GETTING CRITIQUED

A very helpful thing for a songwriter is to have someone else, especially a professional writer or publisher, critique your songs. It can also be one of the most difficult things because our songs are so special to us. Even though it's hard, the goal of a critique is to make the song better and to help you become a better writer.

How to take a critique

When you have the opportunity to be critiqued, remember that songwriting is a learning process. The person critiquing your song was once a new songwriter too. They understand how you feel.

While there can be different opinions about any song, there are basic things the person giving the critique will pay attention to. Here are some things they might talk about:

Is the IDEA relevant, different, and interesting?

Is the LYRIC clear, truthful, focused, and creative?

Is the MELODY singable, current, and memorable?

Does the song have EMOTIONAL IMPACT? Will it make the listener feel the desired emotion?

Is the song COMMERCIAL Could the song compete with other songs on the radio or be on an artist's album?

How you respond to a critique is very important. We all want to hear that our song is perfect. But it is important to be able to listen, take in what is said, and then consider what the person giving the critique tells you. It would be easy to get your feelings hurt, to tell yourself the person doesn't understand or doesn't know what they are talking about. It's even easy to get angry.

Remember that the critiquer is not judging you as a person. They are only talking about your song. The best thing to do when you receive a critique is to be teachable and remember that the person giving the critique is trying to help you be a better writer.

Here are some words you might hear when you have a song critiqued:

Commercially Viable - The song is the kind that people would listen to on the radio or pay money to own.

Dated - The song sounds like something that was popular years ago, but not currently.

Engaging - The song is interesting to the listener.

Focused - The song stays on one topic.

Fresh - The song sounds current and new.

Hooky - There's a part of the melody or lyric that gets stuck in the listener's mind and stays there.

Insightful - The lyric brings out a truth in an interesting way.

Marriage of the lyric and melody - The lyric and melody seem to fit each other well.

Payoff - The hook or the end of the chorus has a big impact because of what it says or the way it says it.

Predictable - The listener can see or hear where the song is going so easily that the song is boring.

Relevant - What the lyric says matters to many people.

Tweak - A fix of the melody or lyric that is just a small change.

Vague - The meaning is confusing or unclear.

Wandering - The melody or lyric doesn't have a clear focus or destination.

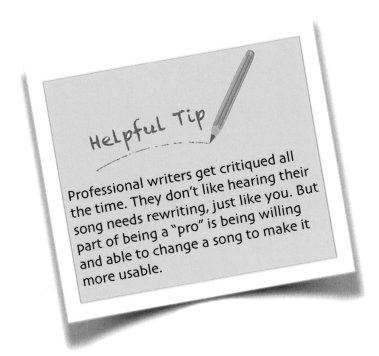

Helpful Tip

Professional writers get critiqued all the time. They don't like hearing their song needs rewriting, just like you. But part of being a "pro" is being willing and able to change a song to make it more usable.

TRY IT OUT

1. Take one of your own songs and rewrite it just for practice. Make changes in the both the lyric and the melody. Change the tempo, the "feel" (if it's a happy melody, see what happens if you make it sound serious or sad). Change the chord progression. See what happens when you are creative enough and brave enough to change what you've written. There is more information about chord progressions at adventuresinsongwriting.org.

2. Get one of your songs critiqued. Send it to the Adventures In Songwriting web site and ask for some feedback about what you've written. What does the critique tell you that you are doing well? What does the critique tell you about areas you still need to work on?

Chapter 9

The Business of Songs

The Facts About How Songwriters Get Paid

Right now you are just learning to write. But one of these days, if you keep at it, you may be writing songs that other people will want to record. That's where this chapter comes in. It's about some basics of the business of songwriting.

How do people make money writing songs?

Most often money is made through royalties. There are laws that govern the use of songs.

When a song gets played on the radio, a performance royalty gets paid to a performing rights organization (PRO). Songwriters are members of a PRO, and this organization collects and distributes these performance royalties to its members.

When a song is recorded on a cd and sold, there is a mechanical royalty that is paid to the writers. The royalties are collected by a publisher or a company that administers songs for independent writers.

ROYALTY
This is the money paid to the songwriter for the use of a song, whether it is through the sale of a cd or a download or for playing the song on radio or TV.

COPYRIGHT
The legal right of ownership of any creative work, for example, a song. The legal owner has the right to print, publish or perform the work or to give others permission to do this in exchange for payment of a royalty.

PUBLISHER
A company or person whose job it is to find ways for a writer's songs to be used and to obtain payment for those uses.

PRO (PERFORMING RIGHTS ORGANIZATION)
For songwriters, the PRO's they are most likely to belong to are:
ASCAP
(American Society of Composers, Authors, and Publishers)
BMI
(Broadcast Music, Inc.)
SESAC
(once stood for Society of European Stage Authors and Composers, but now just goes by SESAC)
SOCAN
(Society of Composers, Authors and Music Publishers in Canada)

If you don't have a publisher to work with, at some point, you may want to protect your rights to your songs. This is called "registering your copyright." It can all be done online at: http://www.copyright.gov. The web site will walk you through registering step by step, and with your parents' help, you'll be able to do it. It's not so important when you are just getting started. It costs money to register a copyright, and so some writers wait until they have a list of songs and register them all at once for one fee.

HERE'S THE MOST IMPORTANT THING:

As a songwriter, you should be a champion of other songwriters. We all have to stick together. That means you understand the value of songs and you help your friends understand it as well. You don't illegally make copies of songs and pass them around. Imagine how you would feel if someone came into your room, went through your belongings, and took the things they liked.

That's how songwriters feel when their songs are taken and used by people who don't pay for them.

Just think of how people "use" songs. We listen while we are waiting in a line or for a plane or at the doctor's office, or just to pass the time.

We listen to make us feel better, to distract us, to lift our spirits when we are sad, to remind us of a good memory, to celebrate special occasions, to persuade someone to buy a product, and even to make someone fall in love.

Songs are important and valuable, and the songs you write as you get better and better will have value.

So be a good member of the songwriting community and raise your voice in support of other songwriters. One day you will want them to do the same thing for you.

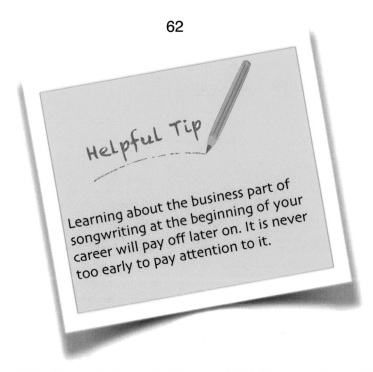

Helpful Tip

Learning about the business part of songwriting at the beginning of your career will pay off later on. It is never too early to pay attention to it.

TRY IT OUT

1. Visit some of the Performing Rights Organization web sites to discover the resources that are available there. You could start at: ascap.com and bmi.com. Read about what these organizations do for songwriters.

2. Read about the different kinds of royalties that songwriters are paid. Here's one good place to start:

http://entertainment.howstuffworks.com/music-royalties1.htm

CHAPTER 10

STOCKING YOUR TOOLBOX

A Few Things That Will Help You As You Write

When a carpenter starts to work on a new project, the most important thing they can do is make sure to have a fully stocked toolbox. They want to be sure everything they need is close by and ready to be put to use. You've learned about a few of the tools needed to write songs. Now here are a few more to help you really live your life like a songwriter.

STORAGE SYSTEM

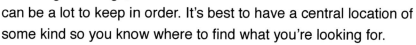

If a carpenter has a lot of tools, but no place to store them all, chances are they are going to have a hard time keeping track of them. It's the same way with songwriters. With all of our ideas for songs, song starts, completed lyrics, and recordings of songs, there can be a lot to keep in order. It's best to have a central location of some kind so you know where to find what you're looking for.

If you want to take the old-fashioned approach to writing, having a notebook devoted to songwriting is helpful. If you're more likely to write on a computer, have some folders devoted to all those ideas, lyrics, and melodies you collect. A smart phone can be a great place to store ideas on a note-taking app, and you can sing your melody ideas into a voice recorder app.

PLANNER

All of us have the same 24 hours in every day, and those hours can get filled up pretty quickly with school, family, activities, church, and time with friends. By setting aside a certain time to write, you create a habit that will serve you well for years to come.

Maybe you like to spend a few minutes writing after school or before you go to bed. Maybe Saturday mornings are the best time for you. Whenever it is, make it a regular time for you to write songs, listen to music, read, or do anything else that focuses your attention on things that make you feel creative.

BOOKSHELF

Writers are readers. Reading is a great way to expand your vocabulary, improve your imagination, and become familiar with a variety of topics. You may have a favorite kind of book – fiction, non-fiction, fantasy, science fiction, biography – but it's a good idea to branch out every once in a while and read something you wouldn't normally pick up. Stories of all kinds are inspiring and can always spark a new song idea.

INSTRUMENTS

Maybe you play an instrument already, but if not, it would be a good idea to start learning how to play something. Piano or guitar would be a great place to start for songwriting purposes. Becoming familiar with as

many instruments as possible will give you more tools to work with in the songwriting process, especially as you think about recording your songs. With each new instrument you learn, you'll open a new door to be creative in a whole new way.

WORD HELPERS

Sometimes you have an idea of what you want to say, but you just can't find the right words to say it. That's when a dictionary, thesaurus, or rhyming dictionary can be very

helpful. You can keep these with you in book form, or they are easily found online. Here are some recommended websites:

Dictionary.com

Rhymezone.com

Rhymebrain.com

Thesaurus.com

LOCATION

This is a different kind of tool for songwriting that some people find important, while others may not. It might help to have a certain place to do your writing. That could be your bedroom or another room in your house. Maybe there's a coffee shop or park where you like to hang out. Creative people like to work in an environment that makes them feel creative. So if you feel most comfortable in a familiar place that has the lighting, temperature, furniture, and anything else that makes you feel more creative, then try making that a regular place for you to write. However, don't get so comfortable in your surroundings that you don't shake things up a little and write somewhere else from time to time.

Stocking your toolbox is an important step in becoming a more productive songwriter. It doesn't have to happen overnight, and it isn't nearly as expensive as stocking a carpenter's toolbox. Little by little, tool by tool, you can fill up your toolbox with the things you'll need to keep writing great songs.

TRY IT OUT

1. Go through the recommended list of tools and write down any that you still need to get for your toolbox. Make a plan for how and when you'll get your toolbox stocked.

2. Create a songwriting spot for yourself somewhere in your house. It could be in a corner of your room, a corner of the garage, or a place in your basement.

CHAPTER 11

LIVING THE ADVENTURE

Habits That Turn You Into A Real Songwriter

Experienced songwriters know that living the songwriting life is fun and interesting, but they know it also means working hard. They know that learning how to write great songs is a life-long challenge. Great songwriters are never finished learning, working, and growing. If you're reading this book, it's a good sign that you already understand that you have a lot to learn. Successful songwriters would tell you that you will never learn it all. What a privilege and responsibility we have.

If you want your songs to have an impact on people, and if you want to use your songwriting to express how you feel about the world and life, the best thing you can do is to keep working at getting better.

So keep writing songs. Keep learning and growing. Keep stretching yourself to try new things.

Time to Write

PLAN YOUR WRITING TIME

Think about your time this way: Approach everything you do, see, and hear, remembering that you are a songwriter. What you are learning at school is important to your writing, whether it's in language classes, history, math, science, art, or music. Look at everything as possible material for your songs or ways to improve your writing.

Regularly spend time simply writing. That could mean that you make appointments with yourself or with co-writers so that you will not let days and weeks go by without spending some time writing.

KEEP AT IT

Sometimes you will get discouraged. You'll feel like you're working hard without a lot of success. But there will be other times when you'll see good things coming in your writing. Whatever happens, if you have a passion to write, keep going. Every professional songwriter has stories about spending a long time before their songs were recorded and heard by others.

LISTEN LIKE A WRITER

Remember that every song you listen to is an opportunity to learn. Develop the habit of listening like a writer. If there is a song you enjoy, ask yourself what works in the song and why. If there's a song that you don't like, analyze what is bothering you about it.

Write down the lyric and analyze what the writer did or didn't do so well. What's going on in the structure of the song? What inventive rhymes and word pictures and expressions did the writer use? What's the big idea of the song? How did the writer get you to that idea? How are the melodic hook and the lyric hook used? How has the writer used repetition and contrast both in the melody and the lyric?

Figure out the chord progression and learn to play the song. There may be ways in the future that you can use a chord progression by altering it, turning it around, changing the time signature—there are many ways you can adapt chords and melodies to make it new.

KEEP LEARNING

If this is your first songwriting book, don't let it be your last. Keep studying and learning from others. Read books about writing, watch documentaries about the lives of songwriters, and when you can, attend workshops and classes.

BUILD COMMUNITY

You can write songs all on your own, but you will find that writing is more fun and you will be more productive if you have a group of songwriting friends. They will be there for you when you get discouraged, there to share your successes, to give you feedback about your songs, and to hold you accountable when you are lazy with your writing. It's important that you are there for your fellow songwriters too.

If you know others who are excited about songwriting, consider starting a songwriting group, either at your school, your church, or independently. Plan regular meetings, invite guest speakers, study through songwriting books together, listen to each other's songs, and best of all, write together.

If you don't know other songwriters close to you, the internet makes it possible for you to connect using platforms like Skype or Google Hangouts. Be sure to do this in a smart, safe way, and always with your parents' permission and supervision.

Our site, adventuresinsongwriting.org is a good place to start.

GREAT SONGWRITERS SAY:

Performing is the easiest part of what I do, and songwriting is the hardest. *—Neil Diamond*

For me, songwriting is something like breathing: I just do it. But that doesn't mean you're fantastic. *—Adam Duritz*

My songs are basically my diaries. Some of my best songwriting has come out of times when I've been going through a personal nightmare. *—Gwen Stefani*

My favorite songwriting trick is writing something like "XO." In my brain, I thought, "This is probably going to be a love song. How can I change that and find ways to twist that?" As a songwriter, it's your job for the song to take twists and turns that people don't expect. *—Kelsea Ballerini*

It's true when they say songwriting is 10% inspiration and 90% perspiration. In truth, what happens is... songs come through you. *—Greg Lake*

Songwriting's never been a natural art for me; it's always been a bit of a struggle. *—Rod Stewart*

Songwriting is my gift from God. *—Smokey Robinson*

I think songwriting is the ultimate form of being able to make anything that happens in your life productive. *—Taylor Swift*

As far as songwriting, my inspirations came from love, life and death, and viewing other people's situations. *—Ed Sheeran*

The rule of songwriting: say what you want to say, say it again, say it a different way, then say it again. *—Hunter Hayes*

A fan once said to me, "Girl, you make me see pictures in my head!" and I took that as a great compliment. That's exactly my intention. *—Joni Mitchell*

The great composer does not set to work because he is inspired but becomes inspired because he is working. Beethoven, Wagner, Bach and Mozart settled down day after day to the job at hand. They didn't waste time waiting for inspiration. *– Ernest Newman*

I do keep little scraps and I think writing-wise I'm probably more of a quilter than a weaver because I get a little scrap here and a little scrap there and I sew them together. *—Rich Mullins*

Songwriting is my way of channeling my feelings and my thoughts. Not just mine, but the things I see, the people I care about. My head would explode if I didn't get some of that stuff out. *—Dolly Parton*

For a songwriter, you don't really go to songwriting school; you learn by listening to tunes. And you try to understand them and take them apart and see what they're made of, and wonder if you can make one, too. *—Tom Waits*

If you pour your life into songs, you want them to be heard. It's a desire to communicate. A deep desire to communicate inspires songwriting. *—Bono*

If you don't have time to read, you don't have the time—or the tools to write. Simple as that. *—Stephen King*

TRY IT OUT

1.Make a list of people you know who are interested in writing songs. Talk with them about starting a songwriting group.

2. Start your own collection of quotes by great songwriters. This is easy to do by Googling "songwriting quotes."

GOT QUESTIONS?

How To Be Part of Our Songwriting Community

After you've had a chance to read this book, you may have questions. Whether it's about something in the book that you didn't understand or it's something else about songwriting that we didn't cover, we would love to hear from you.

Send your questions to us at:

questions@adventuresinsongwriting.org

If you want to get feedback from other songwriters, share your questions on the Adventures In Songwriting web site:

adventuresinsongwriting.org

ACKNOWLEDGEMENTS

We Want To Say Thank You To These People

Thank you to the educators, songwriters, publishers, and mentors who have taught me so much about writing songs; I am grateful for your investment in my creative life. To my family, for faithful encouragement. And to Sue, for being my co-writer, my mentor, and my friend.

—**Gina**

Thank you to Allie and Nick Lapointe, who were inspired to start Kids Write About Jesus in 2014; to my dear friend Gina, who emailed me one day and said, "We should write a songwriting book for kids;" to Johnathan Crumpton, for being my champion for 20 years; to Luke Gambill at Brentwood Benson Songs, who has given me opportunities to write musicals that encourage kids; and to all the young writers who have been part of K-WAJ and moved Gina's heart and mine to write this guide.

—**Sue**

THE WRITERS OF THIS BOOK

Who We Are And What We've Done

GINA BOE

Gina is a songwriter, artist, lover of songs, and developer of people. She has over 30 years experience in the music business with 12 independent recordings, a Dove award, two #1 songs, and cuts by artists such as Mandisa, Group 1 Crew, The Martins, The Talley Trio, Brian Free and Assurance, the Booth Brothers, and many others, as well as several musicals for both adults and children. As the Chief Creative Officer for EnCorps Creative, Gina has written and produced various projects for organizations to use music to communicate their message. She has released two projects for Kids Corps Music, whose mission is to raise up an army of songs for kids. Gina lives in Hickman, NE, with her husband, Perry, four kids, Hunter, Hannah, Harrison and Houston, two dogs, Jake and Gus, and a cat, Leo.

SUE C. SMITH

Sue is a five-time Dove-award winning songwriter who has written 15 #1 songs and over 80 musicals that are sung around the world each year by choirs of all ages. She has twice been named Songwriter of the Year at the Absolutely Gospel Awards and is the co-writer of the Singing News 2016 Song of the Year. She is a staff writer with Capitol Christian Music Group and Daywind Music Publishing. Sue and her husband John founded the Write About Jesus Workshop in 2000 and since then, she has mentored and helped hundreds of writers take the next steps in their songwriting careers. Sue lives in St. Charles, MO, with her husband and a dachshund named Buddy. She has 3 grown children and 8 grandchildren.

Made in the USA
Middletown, DE
10 December 2018